KU-472-601

MATE'S ILLUSTRATED GUIDE TO LUTON

MATE'S ILLUSTRATED GUIDE
TO
LUTON
1907

CHANTRY PRESS

INTRODUCTION © John G. Dony M.B.E. Ph.D.

First published in 1907 by
W. MATE AND SONS LTD.

This second edition published in 1986 by
CHANTRY PRESS (WAKEFIELD) LTD.
3, STATION ROAD,
EARLSHEATON,
DEWSBURY, WEST YORKSHIRE, WF12 8LZ

ISBN: 0 948742 03 8

Chantry Press Ltd wish to thank Dr. John G. Dony and
the staffs of Bedfordshire County Library and Luton Museum and
Art Gallery for their help in the preparation of this edition.

Printed by
THE MOXON PRESS
Morley, Leeds.

INTRODUCTION

Mate's Illustrated Guide to Luton is important in having been originally published in 1907 at a critical turning point in the town's development. In the previous hundred years Luton had grown from a very small town with only about 3,000 inhabitants to one with more than 40,000. Its population had doubled in the last 30 years. The town's continued prosperity had been due entirely to the success of the hat industry, which was still its only one of any consequence. Interesting as this may have been it was not entirely to the comfort of the Town Council, many of whose members were prosperous hat manufacturers, who feared that even a partial collapse of the hat industry would bring distress to the town for which they had a genuine affection. They felt that some means must be found to attract other industries to the town. The full potential of electricity had not yet been realised in 1907, but the Council had put its faith in this as a possible solution to their problems. At a time when most towns were content to depend on 'light and power companies' they embarked on a municipally-owned under-taking, determined to provide electricity as cheaply as it was possible to do so, any profit going to the relief of the already low rates. Cheap power, low rates and a relative nearness to London could be attractive baits for new industries.

The plan had succeeded to the extent that the Guide was able to record the actual or impending arrival of Vauxhall Motors from London; the Davis Gas Stove Company which brought much of its labour force from far away Falkirk; and Commercial Cars which eventually became absorbed into the Renault organisation. George Kent Ltd., specialising in the manufacture of scientific instruments, and Skefko were soon to follow. These five important firms had been attracted to the town in the short period of six years, all being relatively small when they first arrived but soon to grow. For good or ill the face of Luton was beginning to change.

The Guide deals fully with the hat industry, which on the eve of World War I was at its prime but in the years that followed was to suffer a minor decline, just as the Town Council feared it might in the course of time. Nevertheless, thanks to the newly arrived industries the town suffered less in the inter-war depression than many others.

Its population had doubled in the 30 years prior to the publication of the Guide and was to do so again in the corresponding years that followed.

Lutonians of my vintage will find much in the Guide to interest them. They will recall the somewhat hesitant purchase by the Town Council in 1904 of Wardown, with its magnificent Mansion. In a very short time it became the pride of the town, providing at last somewhere to go other than to walk the streets of Luton. The Guide allows us to see these as they last were before the arrival of the trams in 1908 (almost needless to say a municipal service). The main thoroughfares of the town were never to be the same again.

The Guide itself is authoritative and well written, containing much useful as well as nostalgic information. Many readers may find the advertisements, most of which are illustrated, of considerable interest. They recall the days when most shops and businesses were still privately owned by persons who were in many cases respected in the town. These were the days when people were known for their occupations and for the church they attended. It was a closely knit community. An unusual example of this may be seen in the Guide in the advertisement of the private Luton High School for Girls in which the only qualification of the assistant principal is given as 'the daughter of the Revd. W. G. Hutton' – I find it, however, a little strange that I do not remember him. In passing it may be noted that the school did not last long as it could not be expected to compete with the Modern School which in 1904 had at long last brought secondary education to Luton, yet another aspect of progress at this time.

The social historian will find in the Guide an accurate description of a town on the brink of change. After a lapse of only 80 years many of the once prominent buildings are no longer in existence and only one of general scenery (New Bedford Road) still remains unchanged. This will be to the regret of many readers who might wish that Luton could have remained smaller than it is today.

John G. Dony M.B.E., Ph.D.
Luton, February 1986

CHARLES BIRD (COLLINGDON ST.), LUTON.

Telephone No. 55, Luton.

Telegrams—"Paperhangings, Luton."

CHARLES·BIRD. GLASS & LEAD MERCHANT COLLINGDON STREET LUTON

FORWARDING DEPT.

VIEW FROM G.N.R.

GENERAL WAREHOUSE.

WALL PAPER DEPT.

GENERAL WAREHOUSE.

SANITARY GOODS DEPARTMENT.

GALVANISED·CORRUGATED·IRON. WIRE·NETTING. TANKS & CISTERNS. TUBES, PUMPS. PLUMBERS GOODS &c.

UNDERGROUND VARNISH & COLOR DEPT.

Views of some of the Departments in the Extensive Warehouses situated in Collingdon Street,

CHARLES BIRD (COLLINGDON ST.), LUTON.

Telephone No. 55, Luton.   Telegrams—"Paperhangings, Luton."

Exterior view of the Showrooms, adjoining the Warehouses.

MRS. BAKER,

Milliner, ❧
Ladies' and Children's
❧ Outfitter,

GEORGE STREET AND
WELLINGTON STREET,

LUTON, BEDS.

❧

Wedding and Mourning
Orders receive special
❧ attention. ❧

SPECIALISTS IN HIGH-CLASS
PERMANENT ENLARGEMENTS.

All Photos in this
Guide taken by
Mr. Anderson.

A. J. Anderson & Co.,

Photo Artists.

Fine Art Dealers.

Depot for Winsor & Newton's Artists' Materials.

Makers of all kinds
of Picture Frames.

FUMED and
STAINED OAKS,
ENGLISH GOLD,
and THREE PLY
OAKS in
ORIGINAL DESIGNS.

STUDIOS— **37, Wellington St., Luton,**
and at High Street, Leighton, Buzzard.

Fredk. Wood & Co.,

NAT. TELEPHONE NO. 119.

Builders and Contractors.

We are in a position to carry out Large Contracts, our Works being equipped with the latest Machinery, Electrically Driven.

SHOP FRONTS AND OFFICE FITTINGS IN HARD OR SOFT WOODS A SPECIALITY.

Cardiff Grove & Grove Rd., LUTON.

S. Farmer & Co.

PIANO AND :: ::
ORGAN MERCHANTS.

Sole District Agents for **BECHSTEIN, BRINSMEAD, CHAPPELL, ROGERS, CRAMER, SQUIRE, B., BROOKLYN, WALDEMAR**

❧ PIANOS. ❧

3, West St., Dunstable.

2, Wellington St., Luton.

Sole Agents for the **Pianola and the Orchestrelle.**

REPAIRS AND RENOVATIONS by Thoroughly Competent Workmen from the London Houses.

TUNING A SPECIALITY BY QUALIFIED MEN. All parts of the District visited regularly.

SHOW ROOMS :

2, Wellington St. and 85, George St., LUTON.

Branch :—3, **WEST STREET, DUNSTABLE.**

1,000 Stoves, Ranges, Wood, Marble and Slate Mantels.

Largest and best-selected Stock.

Chapel Street.

* * * * *

Special Showroom for

Furnishing Ironmongery,

34, George Street.

THE PRINCIPAL ADDRESS.

GAS FITTINGS a speciality.

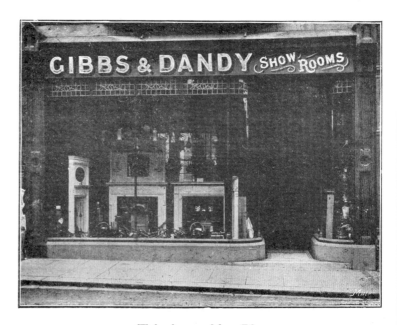

Telephone No. 79.

The Premier Furnishing Establishment

of the District.

UNRIVALLED FOR VALUE AND SELECTION.

REMOVALS AND WAREHOUSING.

Telephone 0689.

Market Hill, and Chapel Street, LUTON.

J. W. GREEN, Ltd., THE BREWERY, LUTON.

**Celebrated Lutonian
Pale & Mild Ales & Stout,**

In Cask and Bottle.

Special Attention and Prompt
Delivery given to Family
Trade Orders.

**Aerated Waters supplied
in Syphons and Corked
Bottles.**

PRICE LIST ON APPLICATION.

Brewery and
Head Office: **Park Street West.**

Telephone No. 122.

J. W. GREEN, Ltd., THE BREWERY, LUTON.

Bonders and Importers of
Choice Old and Well Matured

Scotch & Irish Whiskies

and Genuine COGNAC BRANDIES.

Old Vintage Ports.

A large Selection of

Champagnes, Clarets, Sherries,

and all kinds of

Wines and Liqueurs

kept in Stock.

—

PRICE LIST ON APPLICATION

WINE VAULTS AND MINERAL WATER FACTORY:

- Castle Street. -

SHOWROOM—INTERIOR.

SHOP—INTERIOR.

Choice and
Reliable
Goods
and
Value
Unequalled.

E. Strange
and
Sons,

40, 42 and 44,
Wellington Street,

— Luton.

SHOP—EXTERIOR.

THE DRESS HOUSE.
Household Linens,
Flannels & Blankets,
Lace Curtains, etc.
Choice Blouse Materials,
the Latest Materials at
Popular Prices.

Jackets and Mantles,
Ribbons and Laces,
Gloves and Hosiery,
Corsets and Underclothing,
Umbrellas.

* * * * * * *   *

F. MERCHANT and SONS,

Complete House Furnishers and Removal Contractors.

MOTTO:
"KEEP MOVING."

Blinds
Curtains
Carpets
Linoleums
Bedsteads
Bedding.

Furniture
Stored

IN GOOD DRY STORES.

Furniture
Ironmongery
Trunks
Bags
Draperies
Cabinet
Makers
Upholsterers.

Furniture
Removed

BY EXPERIENCED
WORKMEN.

The
"Luton" Electric Carpet Beating Works,

8 & 10, Manchester St., Luton.

ALEXANDER & SON,

33, WELLINGTON STREET,
—— LUTON. ——

Drapers, Dressmakers, Lacemen & Furriers.

MANTLES AND UNDERCLOTHING.

Established 1889.   Enlarged 1904.

This Establishment is well known in Luton and has a Reputation for Good Class Articles at Moderate Prices.

The . . .
DRESSMAKING DEPARTMENT
is an important feature,
Ladies may rely on both
STYLE AND FIT.

We make the
FUR TRADE
a special study.

COSTUMES, COATS, SKIRTS AND BLOUSES.

═══ **HOUSEHOLD LINENS.** ═══

N.B.—Old Fashioned and Out-of-date Jewellery,
also Old Gold and Silver
taken in exchange or bought for Cash.

The very best value in all
kinds of

**Gold and Silver
Jewellery,** ✄

Silver & Electro Plate,

**Diamond and
Gem Rings**

obtainable in the town is
at the
OLD ESTABLISHED SHOP
of

W. J. BUTCHER

8, Bute Street.

Established 1862.

Best selected stock of
Wedding, Keeper, and Gem Rings,
at Lowest Possible Prices.

DRESSMAKING EXPERTS. . . .
HY. GIBBONS & SON,

PATTERNS
SENT
POST FREE

For : : :
Reliable Dress Fabrics.

DENMARK HOUSE,
 **Luton.**

MATE'S ILLUSTRATED GUIDES.

✳

BOURNEMOUTH:
Printed and Published by
W. MATE & SONS, Ltd.,
Newspaper, Guide Book and
General Publishers,
Art Printers, Etc.

LONDON:
E. MARLBOROUGH & Co.,
51, Old Bailey, E.C.

MANCHESTER:
ABEL HEYWOOD & SON,
Oldham Street.

✳

ALL RIGHTS RESERVED.
COPYRIGHT.

MATE'S ILLUSTRATED LUTON.

1907.

OFFICIAL GUIDE
OF THE
LUTON TOWN
COUNCIL.

✳

— A PICTORIAL AND —
DESCRIPTIVE SOUVENIR

Written by
HUGH ATKINS, B.A.,
(Lond.)

✳

Beautifully Illustrated with
over Thirty Reproductions
from Copyright Photographs
by A. J. Anderson & Co.,
Luton.

E. Deacon & Sons,

Watchmakers, Jewellers,
Fancy Goods Merchants,
Fancy Drapers and : :
Glass and China Dealers.

AGENTS
FOR
GOSS
CHINA.

Fancy Goods and Jewellery Departments.

Glass, China and Fancy Drapery Departments.

—— **HOLD AN IMMENSE STOCK** ——
OF

Jewellery, Clocks, Watches, Leather Goods,
Toys, Dolls, Stationery, Fancy Drapery,
Wools, Silks, Glass, China, Earthenware,
etc., etc.

3, 5, 7, & 9, Wellington Street,

24 & 26, George Street,  **LUTON.**

General Index.

"THE GEORGE" HOTEL, Family and Commercial, Luton.

Proprietor - - - W. E. DIPPLE.

Large Commercial
and
Coffee Rooms.

*

Well-appointed
Billiard Room,
2 Tables.

*

Stock Rooms.

*

Moderate Charges.

Good
accommodation for
Motors.

*

Loose Boxes for
Hunters.

*

Carriages of every
description on hire.

*

Omnibus meets
Trains.

*

TELEPHONE 0654.

WINE & SPIRIT STORES adjoining Hotel.   Large Stock of well-matured Wines & Spirits.

Photo by A. J. Anderson & Co., Luton. **Park Road, Luton.**

Mate's Illustrated Luton.

INTRODUCTION.

No apology is needed for presenting to the public this little Guide to the interesting town of Luton. It will we believe, serve a useful purpose, and secure for itself an appreciative welcome. The letterpress is from the pen of Mr. Hugh Atkins, B.A. (Lond.), and is interesting reading, whilst the illustrations, which are from copyright photographs from the Studios of Messrs. A. J. Anderson & Co., reveal, as no letterpress could do, the characteristic beauties of Luton and the surrounding district. Every endeavour has been made by the Publishers to ensure the accuracy of all particulars in this edition of "Illustrated Luton," but publishers are, after all, only mortal and it is possible errors may all unnoticed have crept into the manuscript; should this be so readers will greatly oblige by pointing out any such inaccuracies to the Editor, 62, Commercial Road, Bournemouth.

W. MATE & SONS, LTD.,

Publishers.

Nat. Telephone No. 58.

Telegrams—"POWDRILL, LUTON."

GEORGE POWDRILL,

1 & 3, HITCHIN ROAD, LUTON.

COAL, COKE, SALT, and BUILDING MATERIAL MERCHANT.

Photo by Wm. H. Cox, 90, Castle Street, Luton.

Brakes, Wagonettes, Flys, Traps, Landaus, Cabs, etc., at short notice.

Largest Haulage Contracts in the County.

Household Removals to all parts.

MAKER OF THE CELEBRATED

Luton Grey Facing Bricks.

BRICKYARDS—

Luton, Cuddington & Dunstable.

MATE'S
ILLUSTRATED LUTON.

EW towns in the Midlands have undergone greater changes and made more rapid progress than Luton during the last thirty years. This applies not only to public improvements, but also to the remarkable development of the staple trade, and Luton's expansion as a busy, commercial centre. The population, which is now about 40,000, and the largest in the county, has doubled since the town was incorporated in 1876. The aspiration contained in its motto: *Scientiæ et labori detur* ("May it be given to skill and industry") has been amply fulfilled, and everyone is agreed that there is a big future for Luton.

In 1801, the population was 3,095, and the maltings and watermills on the Lea were perhaps more important than the plait trade. The respected Town Clerk (Mr. G. Sell), who has a record of 46 years' public service, can recall the days when the chief residences were in the main street, which was banked up on each side.

The magic wand of commerce, with its attendant progress and prosperity, has changed all this. Factories and warehouses of imposing elevation cover considerable areas in the centre of the town, while smart shops of the most modern type abound. The smoke and grime, associated with northern manufacturing towns, is unknown in Luton. On the contrary, the streets are remarkably clean, well paved and lighted. The visitor cannot but be struck with the air of business-like activity prevalent and the signs of general well-being. Sportive writers have occasionally made mild fun about Luton as an "Adamless Eden." However, the prosaic census returns showed in 1901 that the fair sex were nothing like "six to one," but only in a majority of 3,540 among a population of 36,404. In other towns, the disproportion is even greater but if, as Londoners aver, Luton has some repute for its pretty girls, the most ungallant critic is disarmed.

Luton is at a distinct advantage in possessing an artistic, healthy and well-paid occupation for the fair sex, as well as half a dozen large engineering works for male operatives. The wage-earning capacity and the standard of comfort among the working classes are thus maintained well above the average in similar towns.

The centre of the town is in a valley between spurs of the Chilterns, and as the height above sea-level is 430 feet, the climate is bracing and invigorating, especially on the surrounding hills. No expense has been spared by the Corporation in making the sanitation perfect, and £40,000 was recently spent on a main drainage and storm water scheme of sufficient capacity for 100,000 people. With the advent of new industries, the town is going ahead fast. In the past six months, plans for 352 new houses were passed and about two miles of streets have been laid out, making a total of 42 miles. The police force of forty are troubled with little serious crime, and last year out of 73 prosecutions for drunkenness, 40 were against tramps and outsiders. The district for miles round abounds in pretty scenery, to which access is easy for all who drive, cycle or motor along main roads of excellent surface, for which Bedfordshire is famed.

Civic Luton.

THE Town Council comprises a Mayor, six Aldermen, and eighteen Councillors. As a borough, Luton is one of the best equipped and administered in the Kingdom, and its finances are in a particularly sound condition. The spirit of enterprise and progress has always been tempered with wise economy. The outstanding loans of the Corporation amount to the moderate sum of £175,405, which is more than balanced by substantial assets in the electricity undertaking, Council Schools, and extensive freeholds in buildings and lands, covering a total area of 200 acres.

The Town Hall, built in 1847, was acquired in 1874, and the Council have since purchased considerable property adjoining it, their intention being to erect a new Town Hall and Municipal Offices on this ideal site in due course. The Corn Exchange, opened in 1869, occupies the site of the old market house.

The Plait Halls in Cheapside and Waller Street, erected in 1868, are now free from debt and a source of income, the former being used for plait storage, and the latter for public meetings and entertainments.

The Corporation Free Library, opposite the Town Hall, contains 5,000 volumes. It was erected by subscription and afterwards purchased by the Council, who adopted the Free Libraries Act in 1894.

The Highways Depot of the Corporation is a fine suite of buildings, costing £6,000 and built in 1900, adjoining the electricity station. A new Fire Station was constructed in 1902 in Church Street, and has the latest equipments. All members of the Brigade are in telephonic communication.

An up-to-date Refuse Destructor by Horsfall was completed in March, 1905, at a cost of £6,250. The

Photo by A. J. Anderson & Co., Luton.

Corn Exchange and Market Hill.

9

three cells consume 40 tons of refuse daily. The heat generated is used for the sewage pumping plant and the steam disinfector.

The Corporation's electricity station and public baths are described below. The Court House and Police Station are also owned by the town. It only remains to add that the Luton Corporation Tramways Order was confirmed by Parliament in August, 1905, and various schemes are now being considered.

LOW RATES.

Notwithstanding the immense improvements made in the town, the total rates to-day are only 6s. 6d. in the £. The Town Council is responsible for 3s., which is about 3d. below the past thirty years' average, and the Poor rate (including county and education demands) has been 3s. 6d. for the past three years.

The rateability is £178,000, and the yield of a penny rate, which was £430 in 1897 and £540 in 1902, has increased to £640. Borough rate, £695.

VITAL STATISTICS.

Keen supervision of all sanitary matters and the strict enforcement of building bye-laws have made Luton one of the healthiest of manufacturing towns. The death-rate last year was only 13.6 per thousand, and the mortality from zymotic disease was reduced to .04 per thousand, the lowest figure ever recorded.

Railway Facilities.

LUTON is exceptionally favoured in this respect. It is on the main line of the Midland Railway, and between Luton and London, a distance of 30 miles, there is an excellent service of 35 trains daily, some of which make the journey in forty minutes. The town is also connected by a branch line with the Great Northern Railway at Hatfield and the London and North Western Railway at Leighton Buzzard, both only 12 miles distant. Much of the land available for new industries adjoins the railway lines and the great advantage of having sidings in communication with the main systems is an important point with those establishing works and factories in the town.

The Staple Trade.

THE factories of Luton engaged in the staple trade have an enormous output in a season of all kinds of headgear. The past half century has witnessed a revolution in the industry; first, in the sources from which the raw material is derived; and secondly, in the materials themselves and in the endless variety of manufacture.

Till about 1870, most of the straw plait was made by cottagers in the country districts of Bedfordshire, Herts and Bucks. The plait market in Luton on Mondays used to be the great event of the week, and the main street was crowded with stalls, the purchases

Photo by A. J. Anderson & Co., Luton.

George Street and Ames' Memorial Fountain.

11

by the manager of one of the largest hat factories often exceeding £500 in value. To remove the plait selling from the streets, the Plait Halls were built, but their purpose had only a brief fulfilment, for the rapidly increasing importation of foreign plaits soon began and effected a transformation of the trade. Workers, who were earning at most 5s. to 7s. a week by plaiting straw, found their occupation gone and flocked into the town to engage in the far more profitable business of manufacturing hats. First came fine pedal and eleven-end Tuscan plait from Italy, and then an immense and cheap supply from China, followed by even greater exports from Japan. It is interesting to recall that 17 years ago two Japanese gentlemen were introduced to the Deputy Mayor of Luton (Alderman A. Hucklesby) by Messrs. Manning, Collyer & Co., then the largest Chinese plait brokers, and shown round the Luton Plait Halls. Within 18 months, a consignment of plait arrived from Japan, which for lightness and artistic finish quite surpassed the Chinese and English rustic then in vogue. The first importer of Canton plait was burnt in effigy in Luton market place, but there can be no doubt whatever that the home supply of plait could never have provided more than a fraction of the industry's requirements in its present expansion. By a happy coincidence, the sewing machine came into use in the trade almost simultaneously with the new supplies of raw materials.

At present Japanese plaits, ranging in price from 4d. to 4s. 6d. per piece of sixty yards, are pre-eminent, and constitute the raw material for 60 per cent. of straw hats now made. Moreover, the Japs have successfully copied and beaten the Italians, who were long supreme in certain lines. Chinese fine plaits still find a ready market, Italian pedal holds its own for men's and children's hats, while Swiss fancies and German braids are used in other classes of goods. Despite a recent attempt to revive English plait, it now accounts for barely one per cent. of Luton's output.

At the moment of writing, however, there is a revival, temporarily at least, in the best quality of English split straw, for exportation to the New York market. Possibly English fashion may coincide next season with this movement.

The processes of manufacture in the large factories, many of which use electricity for power and light, are as beautiful and artistic as are the materials employed. In the old days, only a score of shapes were in vogue for a whole season; to-day, a Luton manufacturer often produces 2,000 different designs in hats from the ordinary "boater" to the most elaborate creation for Ascot or Henley. The anticipation and study of fashion is, of course, an important factor.

But Luton's energies are not confined to straw goods. Chiffon, velvet and chenille hats, either semi-trimmed or ready to wear, are a recent innovation of remarkable finish and skill in manufacture. This millinery department of the trade has a big future, and the remarkable progress made of late has resulted in considerable developments among firms supplying materials for trimmings. The new departure in millinery has created another subsidiary trade—that of cartoon makers—in

Photo by A. J. Anderson & Co., Luton.

New Bedford Road.

which ten local houses are engaged. To encourage taste and originality of design, the Chamber of Commerce has instituted an annual hat-trimming competition for girls in the elementary schools. In the autumn, many local firms manufacture ladies' felts, beavers and furs. Large shipping orders are given in Luton for Canada, Australia and the British Colonies, as well as for the Continent and other parts of the world. King Edward and Queen Alexandra have been supplied direct with hats of Luton manufacture.

The bleaching and dyeing of plait has, by scientific methods, been brought to such a pitch of excellence that Luton leads the world in this branch of the industry. The chemical constitution of Luton water is a factor in this success. Some 50,000 bales and cases of plait are despatched to Luton in a year, about 30 per cent. of which is re-exported.

Various conjectures have been made as to the origin of the trade. Shakespeare speaks of rye-straw hats and Pepys' Diary (Hatfield, 1667) mentions "straw hats, which are much worn in this part of the country." No doubt, the fine straw grown on the chalk and flinty soil of this district was particularly suitable for plaiting. When the Prince of Wales, our present King, visited Luton in 1878, and inspected a straw trade exhibition in the Plait Hall, His Royal Highness was presented with an address soliciting his encouragement of the demand for "hats and bonnets of our English-made plaits." The address also stated that the town "owed the introduction into this district of the manufacture of straw plait" to King James I., who "about

the year 1605 placed some Lorraine plaiters (brought over by Mary Queen of Scots) here under the protection of Sir R. Napier, then owner of Luton Hoo." Unfortunately, there seems to be no historical proof of this statement, and the late Mr. John Waller, whose family were the pioneers of the trade in Luton, after giving the results of investigations into parish registers and other documents, describes the story as "a pleasing fiction." There is no mention of the trade at Luton earlier than 1764. For some time, of course, Dunstable was its chief centre, but Luton took the lead about a century ago, and its fame as the metropolis of the straw hat industry has since gone out into all lands.

New Industries.

THE Luton Chamber of Commerce, which has had a very useful career of 30 years and sprung out of the old Plait Measuring Association, takes a prominent position among the Chambers in the Kingdom. In July, it organised a successful visit by Colonial delegates from all parts of the Empire, and in describing this, Mr. Craig-Brown (Vice-President of the Associated Chambers) said : "We have seen what a remarkably clean town, what splendid buildings and what a profitable industry have been made out of straw."

Thanks largely to the work of the New Industries Committee, composed of members of the Chamber of Commerce and the Corporation, Luton is not dependent altogether upon the hat trade, for it has some

Photo by A. J. Anderson & Co., Luton.

The Downs.

15

large engineering and kindred undertakings. The co-operation of the two chief land owners has been secured, and during the past six years, the efforts of this committee, of which Alderman G. Warren is Chairman, and the Town Clerk and Mr. T. Keens (Secretary of the Chamber) are hon. Secretaries, have assisted in the introduction of important new firms. Among them are : The Vauxhall Motor and West Hydraulic Co., Limited, in Kimpton Road ; the Davis Gas Stove Co., who have built extensive works covering six acres in Dallow Road ; the cocoa and chocolate factory of the Co-operative Wholesale Society, Dallow Road; the Motor Works of the Commercial Cars, Limited, Biscot Road ; and the British Gelatine Works, Limited, Bedford Road. Messrs. Hayward, Tyler and Co., makers of hydraulic and pumping machinery, who have been established in Luton 35 years, now employ about 600 hands. Here also notable extensions have been made, as well as at the large boiler works of Balmforth and Co., Limited.

Luton Parish Church.

THE people of Luton may be congratulated upon the possession of what no other parish in the county can boast—a church whose recorded history reaches back more than 800 years. It is the only link of an aggressively modern town with the distant past. Its associations with the Washington and Penn families are noted by Baedeker as appealing to American visitors ; and for the general tourist it is described as the most interesting parish church near London. One of the largest churches in England, it is dedicated to St. Mary, and its history is briefly summarised in the beautiful O'Neill memorial window, which depicts King Athelstan (Saxon founder of the church), Robert, Earl of Gloucester (the Norman founder), John de St. Albans (the first Vicar), and Lord Wenlock, who built in 1461 the chapel in which the window is placed. To students of architecture the church is known as one of the finest specimens in the country of thirteenth to fifteenth century work, its prevailing character being Decorated and Perpendicular. The interior of the church is symmetrically perfect, almost cathedral-like in proportions, and even more imposing in appearance than the exterior.

Many thousands have been spent on the work of restoration, which was begun in 1865 and carried on almost continuously by Mr. O'Neill during his Vicariate of nearly thirty-five years. The present Vicar (the Rev. E. R. Mason) has continued it. The roofs of the nave and transepts, which are richly moulded, and probably date from the time of Henry VIII., have just been renewed at a cost of £2,500. The tower and steeple, one of the best examples of its class of the fourteenth century, is in urgent need of restoration. Great improvements have been effected since the old days, when the beautiful arches of the chancel and nave were blocked by ugly galleries and the oak screens defaced by paint.

A unique feature of the church is the 14th century Baptistery, which was formerly in the south transept

Parish Church, from North Side.

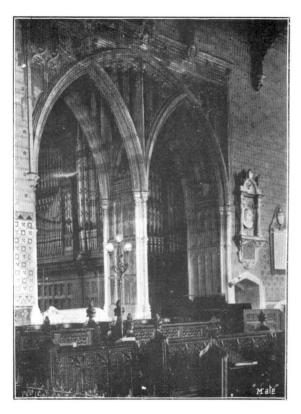

Photo by
A. J. Anderson & Co., Luton.

Gothic Stone Screen,

Showing Preby. Wm. Wenlock's Tomb, the Organ
and Console, and the O'Neill Memorial,

18

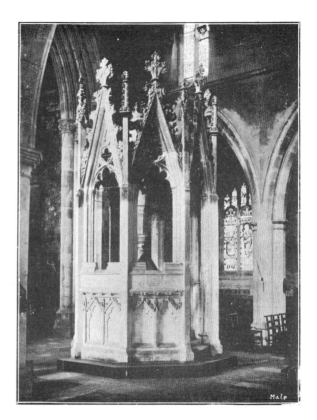

Photo by
A. J. Anderson & Co., Luton.

**The Baptistry,
Luton Parish Church.**

Photo by A. J. Anderson & Co., Luton.

Parish Church : Interior.

and after the restoration was removed to its original position and placed on a base of Isle of Man black marble. A superb structure of Decorated workmanship, octagonal in shape and twenty feet high, it is of white Totternhoe stone, richly carved, and has open traceried panels under crocketed gables, divided from each other by buttresses terminating in pinnacles. The lower panels up to a height of five feet are solid, and enclose the thirteenth century Purbeck marble font, round which there is space for eight persons to stand. The font cover is made of old oak from the belfry. The groined roof has a large boss elegantly carved to represent a lamb guarding a vine from the attacks of a dragon. It is said that there are only two other canopies over fonts in England (at Trunch, Norfolk, and St. Peter Mancroft, Norwich), but both these are of wood and different in other respects. The absurdity of the tradition that Queen Anne Boleyn was the donor of the baptistery is clearly shown by the Rev. H. Cobbe, the erudite author of the "History of Luton Church." The chancel was restored about the middle of the fifteenth century by John of Wheathamstead, a famous Abbot of St. Albans. On the dissolution of St. Albans Monastery in 1539, the advowson of the vicarage and the rectorial tithes passed into the hands of the King. Thus, after a connection of 384 years, Luton ceased to acknowledge the jurisdiction of the Abbots. But a re-union with St. Albans will shortly be brought about by the new diocesan arrangements.

Many changes were made at the east end forty years ago. A new three-light lancet window was given by Mr. Crawley, and over it in opaque mosaics are depicted choirs of angels soaring amid fleecy clouds. The reredos is a remarkably successful representation by Salviati in Venetian mosaics of Da Vinci's fresco of "The Last Supper," the masterpiece of the Florentine school, which is now in the refectory of a convent at Milan. The picture is enclosed in an alabaster frame-work with seven arched canopies and crocketed finials between them. The mosaics are practically imperishable, and the figures stand out with striking clearness from the golden groundwork.

The beautiful groined recess on the south side of the chancel, with the rebus of his name, was erected by Richard Barnard, Vicar from 1477 to 1492, as a chantry. Over the four stone sedilia in the sanctuary are eight shields with coats-of-arms. The arms of Abbot Wheathamstead (now used as the badge of Luton Secondary School) and of William of Wykeham, the great architect-Bishop, appear twice. The others belong to King Offa of Mercia, King Edward the Confessor, Queen Philippa (wife of Edward III.), and St. Albans Abbey. On the north side are a blind Perpendicular window above the Late Decorated Easter sepulchre and the mural tablet, with sculptured medallion portrait by F. W. Pomeroy, erected by the parishioners in memory of Mr. O'Neill. The chancel is separated from the Wenlock chapel by a lofty Gothic double arch or screen, which is considered the finest of its kind in Northern Europe. Coats-of-arms of Lord Wenlock, encircled by the Garter, appear prominently. Beneath the western arch of the screen is a remarkable altar tomb with the

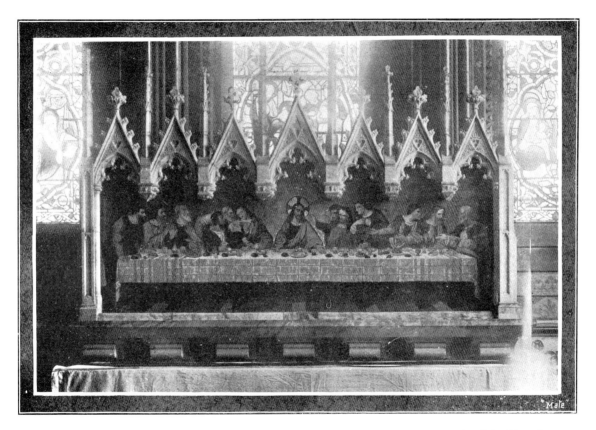

"Male"

Photo by A. J. Anderson & Co., Luton.

**Reredos, Parish Church :
Da Vinci's "Last Supper."**

effigy of William Wenlock, great-uncle of Lord Wenlock, and Master of Farley Hospital, near Luton, from 1377 to 1392. The inscription is one of the very earliest in English, and perhaps the first combining English and Latin. Beneath the eastern arch is the altar tomb of Lady Rotheram, and on the north side of the chapel are those of her son John, the first of the name who possessed Someries, and George Rotheram, lord of the manor. Here also is the traditional burial-place of Thomas Rotheram, Archbishop of York, 1480-1500, and Lord Chancellor to Edward IV. An oak case displays an early edition of Foxe's Book of Martyrs and an old folio Bible.

The earliest brass remaining is that of "Hugo Atte Spetyll" (Spittalsea) in the Wenlock Chapel and dates from the 15th century. The brasses of John Ackworth (lord of the manor of Biscot and founder of the Trinity Guild), 1512, in the north transept, and of John Sylam (of Bramingham) and Dr. Sheffield, Vicar from 1502 to 1526, in the south transept, are also noteworthy.

The oldest monumental relic in the parish is the stone coffin-lid, which occupies an arched recess in the south aisle. The picturesque sacristy, groined in four bays from a central stone shaft, projects some inches beyond the east end. The explanation is that the eastern half of this building was transplanted when Lord Wenlock required part of the site of the old sacristy in erecting his Chantry Chapel. The upper room, which now contains the blowing apparatus of the organ, was used as a school a century ago.

The richly carved oak screens between the Hoo and Wenlock Chapels and the transepts embody some parts of the old rood-screen. The Transitional arch between the south transept and aisle is the most ancient part of the church. The ring and staple to which Coverdale's Bible was attached in 1536 can be seen in the choir stalls. The organ is a splendid instrument of forty stops, rebuilt by Norman and Beard. Space only permits mention of the handsome marble pulpit, presented to Mr. O'Neill after twenty years' work as Vicar; the ten clerestory windows depicting coats of arms of English sees; the fine peal of eight bells, with the Victoria Memorial clock and chimes, by J.W. Benson, Ltd.; and Fuseli's picture of Noah's offering, now hung under the tower and formerly in Lord Bute's gallery.

The Rev. Edmund Robert Mason, M.A., of Queen's College, Oxford, has been Vicar of Luton since April, 1897, and is also Rural Dean and Surrogate.

OTHER CHURCHES.

CHRIST CHURCH, in Upper George Street, is the centre of the largest parish in the town, and was opened in 1857. What was originally a building of poor architectural merit has been much improved, at a total cost of £5,000, by the addition of a decorated Gothic chancel in 1881, an organ by Nicholson, and a new north aisle, vestry and organ chamber in January, 1904. The nave is ultimately to be rebuilt. The late Vicar (the Rev. E. H. Lowe) built the Parish Room on part of the Vicarage grounds, and in addition to this generous

Photo by A. J Anderson & Co., Luton.

Christ Church.

gift, bequeathed £500 for church extension in the parish. The new Vicar is the Rev. C. Morgan Smith, B.D., formerly senior Curate of St. Peter's, Leicester.

St. Matthew's Church, in High Town, is a good specimen of a modern brick church, erected in 1876 at a cost of £5,500, Madame de Falbe (of Luton Hoo) and the Duke of Bedford being munificent contributors. The beautiful reredos of Caen stone with a Sicilian marble cross was given in 1885 in memory of the first Vicar (the Rev. J. Wood) by his widow, the stone pulpit being also presented by the congregation as a memorial. An elegant font was given by Dr. H. Sworder in memory of his wife. The present Vicar is the Rev. H. Coate. Connected with the parish is the Church Army Hall in Brunswick Street.

St. Paul's Church, in New Town, was dedicated by the Bishop of Ely in 1891, and is a lofty brick building of simple Early English style, similar to St. Matthew's. During the Vicariate of the Rev. T. Bulman, a capital organ, with chamber and vestry, have been added, and funds are in hand for building a Vicarage. The Church Army is also working in this parish.

St. Saviour's Church, Russell Street, is a very substantial building with a dignified interior, built from the designs of the late Mr. J. T. Micklethwaite, surveyor to Westminster Abbey. Formerly attached to Christ Church, it became a separate parish in 1893, and the original mission Church is now used as a Parish Room. Viscount Peel laid the foundation stone of the north aisle, which was the first part of the permanent church, in May, 1897. In November, 1904, Adeline, Duchess of Bedford, laid the foundation stone of the nave and chancel, which Bishop Harrison dedicated a year later. The Rev. J. C. Trevelyan has been Vicar since the formation of the parish.

St. Andrew's Mission Church, Crawley Road, was built in 1887 on land given by the late Mr. J. S. Crawley, and a brick chancel was added in 1901. It is attached to Christ Church.

The Mission Hall in Manor Road is worked in connection with the Parish Church.

The Roman Catholics have for twenty years had an iron Church in Castle Street, dedicated to " Our Lady Help of Christians." The Presbytery adjoins the site for the future church. The Rev. Henry O'Connor is the present rector.

Nonconformist Places of Worship.

Besides the five parish churches, there are over twenty places of worship belonging to various sects. Nonconformity has always been exceptionally strong in Luton; indeed, until fifty years ago, the Church of England was only represented by the parish church among 14,000 people.

The Baptists were the earliest Dissenters in Luton. The Old Baptist Meeting House in Park Street, replaced in 1870 by a modern building, dated back to the seventeenth century, and the first pastor, Thomas Marsom,

St. Matthew's Church.

Photo by A. J. Anderson & Co., Luton. **Congregational Church.**

was a fellow prisoner with John Bunyan in Bedford gaol. An old oak chair, which Bunyan is said to have used when he preached at Luton, is preserved in one of the vestries at Park Street Church. The Union Church, Castle Street, which has recently received £345 from Mr. Carnegie for a new organ, was built in 1837, and the Wellington Street Baptist Church in 1847.

Wesleyan Methodists are a very strong body in Luton, and the Chapel Street Church is one of the largest places of worship in Methodism. John Wesley preached six times in Luton and found a staunch supporter in Mr. Wm. Cole, who was at one time High Sheriff, and resided at the Vicarage for some years during Dr. Prior's absence from the parish. Mr. Cole built the first Methodist Meeting House in Church Street, where Wesley preached for the last time in Luton in 1785, and endowed it with £10 10s. a year. Mr. Thos. Hawkes, writing in these early days, said : " Luton Methodists at this time generally attended Church and Sacrament ; there was only preaching at the Methodist Chapel on Sunday evenings." The present Chapel Street Church was opened in 1852 and is the second on that site. It contains a fine organ of 34 stops by Hill and Son. The Waller Street Church dates from 1863 and its members have recently completed a big scheme in the Central Mission Hall, Midland Road, which cost £8,000. Other Wesleyan Chapels are at North Street, Church Street, and Bailey Hill.

The Primitive Methodists, another vigorous body, built their first chapel in High Town over half a century

Photo by A. J. Anderson & Co., Luton.   **Wesleyan Church, Chapel Street.**

ago. They have places of worship in London Road, Church Street, Cardigan Street, Park Town and Dunstable Road.

The Congregationalists have two handsome churches in King Street, with a lofty spire, opened in 1866, and at Bury Park, erected three years ago.

The Friends Meeting House in Castle Street dates from 1799, and the Adult School in Church Street has a widespread influence, over 800 men and women attending the classes on Sundays.

The Salvation Army has two corps in Luton, the Temple in Park Street being a large building. The Particular Baptists worship at Ebenezer Chapel, Hastings Street, and Bethel Chapel, Chapel Street. Special attention is given to Sunday Schools in Luton, and thousands of pounds have been spent in the past two decades on erecting halls and class-rooms for this work. The Plymouth Brethren, Railway Mission and Gospel Missions complete the list of religious agencies.

Hospitals.

THE Bute Hospital was erected in 1882 in Dunstable Road, on land given by the Marquis of Bute, though it was founded ten years earlier as a cottage hospital in High Town. As a memorial of King Edward's Coronation two new wards for 24 beds have been added, and were opened by Lady Wernher in July, 1904. These embody the latest ideas of experts in hospital construction, and the entire cost of over £4,000 has been raised by public subscription. The hospital is equipped with X Rays apparatus and the average number of in-patients is thirty. That the institution has a strong hold on the interest and sympathy of the working classes is shown by the fact that the Hospital Saturday street and factory collections this year reached the record sum of £484. Mr. F. Crawley, J.P., is President; Mr. W. R. Phillips, J.P., Vice-President and Chairman of the Committee; and County Alderman H. O. Williams, J.P., Hon. Secretary.

The Luton Children's Sick and Convalescent Home occupies an elevated position in London Road, and was the generous gift of Mr. A. P. Welch, who was made the first Freeman of the borough. The Home was opened by the Duchess of Bedford in June, 1894. Last year 133 children were admitted, 68 being free cases; most of these were discharged cured, and others were greatly benefited. Dr. H. Sworder rendered devoted service as Medical Superintendent for 16 years, and has been succeeded by Dr. Bone. The place of Mr. R. E. Cooke, who acted as Hon. Secretary since the foundation of the Home, was recently taken by Mr. G. H. Latchmore. The Luton Children's Guild of Kindness has about five hundred members, and has raised nearly £1,400 for the Home and the Hospital since 1895.

The Town Council has an Isolation Hospital for infectious diseases at Spittalsea, an ideal site 500 feet above sea level. This is a curious return to the old order of things, for the spot is named from a hospital once existing near, of which, according to a deed of the 15th century, Thomas à Becket, Archbishop of Canterbury, was the founder.

Photo by A. J. Anderson & Co., Luton.   **Waller Street Wesleyan Church and Wesleyan Hall.**

Education.

THE Luton Secondary School and Technical Institute has for two years been carried on in temporary premises. The County Council have acquired a very central site in Park Square at a cost of £4,000, and about £10,000 will be spent on the new building, which is being erected, and will accommodate 300 pupils. Mr. T. A. E. Sanderson, M.A., scholar of Trinity College, Cambridge, and formerly Bursar and mathematical master of Bath College, is the Principal. The evening classes for technical instruction, include departments for science, art, engineering and commercial subjects and are attended by 600 students.

The institution is fortunate in having as Chairman of the Board of Governors Mr. R. E. Prothero, M.V.O., a distinguished Oxford scholar and man of letters. The fees are £1 10s. a term, and a number of scholarships are available.

The percentage of attendance and standard of instruction at the Luton Elementary Schools has long been among the highest in the Kingdom. There are about 7,500 children on the registers of the seven Council and five non-Council Schools.

ST. GREGORY'S SCHOOL, the Downs, was specially built on an elevated site having extensive views. The curriculum is designed to prepare boys for the public Schools, the Navy, and professional and commercial careers. Mr. W. House, the Principal, is a successful teacher of much experience. Every provision is made for sports in a large playing field, and the school has a particularly good record for swimming.

The LUTON HIGH SCHOOL for Girls and Kindergarten at Lyndhurst, Cardiff Road, has long had a reputation for careful instruction on modern methods. Preparation for musical and local examinations is given by a qualified staff under the direction of Miss Gilfillan, while girls are also trained for secondary school teaching. Ample grounds are attached to the school, which has a field for tennis, hockey and cricket.

ST. DOMINIC'S CONVENT occupies spacious premises at the top of Rothsay Road. It is a High School with Kindergarten and a Boarding School for daughters of gentlemen. Madame la Prioresse and the Sisters, who came from Dijon, hold diplomas for teaching and prepare pupils for public examinations of England and France. Special attention is paid to modern languages. The Convent has a large garden with fine trees.

Wardown: Luton's Pleasure Resort.

THE opening of Wardown, Luton's new public park and pleasure ground, has been the most popular event in the history of the borough. At Whitsuntide, it was estimated that 20,000 people visited the park, and during the summer it has attracted pic-nic parties for miles round. The enterprise of the Town Council has enabled the inhabitants to enjoy the possession of a beautiful estate, laid out at great cost and now practically matured with 30 years' growth of trees and plantations. The original name of the estate was

Photo by *A. J. Anderson & Co., Luton.*

The Mansion, Wardown Park.

Bramingham Shott, but its present appellation, Wardown, which was transferred by Mr. Forder (a former occupier) from one of the Hampshire Downs, near Petersfield, has certainly the merit of historical appropriateness. Just beyond the park and near Great Bramingham are the shallow dykes, known as Dray's Ditches, which extend across the Icknield Way. There is good reason to suppose that these are connected with the ancient encounter between the Danes and the men of Luton in 914.

Wardown has an area of fifty acres, and was developed by Mr. F. C. Scargill, a local solicitor and steward of the Manor of Luton, who erected the mansion in 1877. Much of the land was formerly bog, but, owing to the gradual sinking of the level of springs in the Lea Valley, this state of affairs has disappeared.

When the question of acquiring Wardown from a local syndicate came before the ratepayers' meeting, there was only a majority of 30 in its favour. In September, 1903, the Council decided to purchase for £16,250, a sum said to be less than that spent on the erection of the mansion and buildings alone. About £6,000 has been expended in laying out the park, making the lake and providing bandstand, bridges, boat-house, new bowling green, cricket pitch, etc. The popularity of boating on the lake has exceeded all anticipations, and from April to the end of September the fees for boat hire have amounted to £363. An electric motor is used for pumping water into the lake, when the river Lea takes a subterranean holiday and periodically disappears from view. As the water is only 3ft. 6ins. deep, the immersion of a rash and inexperienced oarsman is not a serious matter and provides a comic interlude for the spectator on dry land. The Parks Committee are already contemplating a scheme for enlarging the lake.

Before Wardown was opened, the old English game of bowls was almost unknown in Luton. The two greens in the park have been thronged with players during the summer, and a Town Bowling Club has been formed among local enthusiasts. The three admirable tennis courts have won much favour, and the fine cricket pitch has given the national pastime a new lease of life in Luton.

The pleasure grounds surrounding the mansion are approached through a delightful avenue of limes, Here the eye feasts on an expanse of velvet lawn, relieved by rich flower beds and bordered by stately trees. Along the walks are

" . . . Seats beneath the shade,
For talking age and whispering lovers made."

Small wonder that Luton people have entered joyously upon their inheritance and opponents of the purchase are silenced. The ground floor of the mansion is used for a refreshment pavilion ; tea and ices are served in the dining room with its verandah overlooking the lawn—a charming spot on a summer day. There are eighteen bed and dressing rooms on the upper floors, which may some day be converted into a museum. The porch at the entrance of the mansion is adorned with busts of Palmerston, Dickens, Cobden, Bright, Disraeli and Gladstone. A large greenhouse enables

Photo by A. J. Anderson & Co., Luton.

The Lake, Wardown Park.

the flower-beds to be constantly replenished. A company of entertainers, the "Zig-Zags," have given musical performances daily during the summer, and local bands have attracted crowds of listeners on Saturday and Sunday evenings.

In connection with the acquisition of the estate by the Corporation, mention should be made of the public spirit of the Mayor (Alderman Hucklesby), Alderman E. Oakley and Councillor A. Oakley, who agreed to share the financial responsibility in the event of the purchase not being completed.

Recreation Grounds.

IT was inevitable that, since the opening of Wardown, the People's Park, which was laid out in 1868 after an exchange of Moor land with Mr. Crawley, should suffer an eclipse of popularity. Nevertheless, the Park has a charming situation on the breezy heights above the town, and affords extensive views. The Bell Close, and part of Pope's Meadow, both adjoining the Park, are used for cricket and football. High Town thus possesses 43 acres of open space. The old Moor, on the west side of the Bedford Road "boulevard," covers five acres. In 1894 the Corporation acquired, at a cost of £7,000, two recreation grounds together of fourteen acres area, in Manor Road and Dallow Road for the population of the East and West Wards respectively. Seats are placed in what was once the Vicarage garden, next to the borough electricity station, as a quiet resort for old folk.

Stockwood Park.

A FAVOURITE walk is up the Lawn-path to Woodside and Slip End through Stockwood Park, the seat of Mr. Francis Crawley, J.P. The Crawley family are the chief landowners round Luton, where they have been established since the reign of Henry VIII., and perhaps earlier. Sir Francis Crawley, a Judge of the Court of Common Pleas, voted for granting the ship-money to Charles I., and his property was sequestered by Parliament for " delinquency in adhering to the King." He married the daughter of Sir John Rotheram, thus succeeding to Someries. His second son Francis was a Baron of the Exchequer, temp. Charles II., and his estates also suffered decimation under the Commonwealth. Both died at Nether Crawley, where was the ancient seat of the family (called Haverings, the site of which is now ploughed over), and were buried in the Wenlock Chapel of Luton Church. The mansion at Stockwood was built by John Crawley, Esq., in 1740. The late Squire, Mr. John Sambrook Crawley, built the churches at Biscot and Woodside.

Someries Castle.

TWO miles south of Luton are the ruins of Lord Wenlock's mansion, which was known a century ago as "Summeris Towers." Here was once the seat of an ancient family, whose most conspicuous member, Roger de Somery, fought against his neighbour, Simon

Photo by A. J. Anderson & Co., Luton.   **The Sands, Wardown Park.**

de Montfort (then lord of the manor of Luton), and the confederate Barons at the Battle of Lewes, 1264. In those days Someries Castle was a complete specimen of a feudal stronghold, fortified with drawbridge and portcullis to defend its occupants against sudden assaults. Lord Wenlock's mansion was begun about the middle of the fifteenth century, and must not be confounded with the original moated Castle, which has disappeared. Portions remain of the chapel at the east-end, and the gateway with chambers on either side, with vestiges of the hall on the western side, originally fifty feet long. There were probably other buildings to the north, and though Lord Wenlock left the mansion unfinished, it was a remarkable example of early brick architecture. Someries Castle has been the property of the owners of Luton Hoo for two centuries, and is occupied with the surrounding farm by Mr. B. Cole.

Luton Hoo.

AMONG the stately homes of England, Luton Hoo is of notable interest and importance. King Edward VII., when Prince of Wales, paid three visits to the Hoo—in 1878, in 1886 (when an address was presented by the Mayor and Corporation of Luton), and in 1889. On the last two occasions His Royal Highness was accompanied by our present Queen Alexandra. The engagement of Princess May and the late Duke of Clarence took place during their stay at Luton Hoo in 1891 as the guests of Madame de Falbe.

Sir Julius C. Wernher, Bart., purchased he mansion and estate three years ago, and became Lord of the Manor of Luton. The interior has since undergone extensive re-construction and renovation; a new storey has been added and electricity installed throughout. Many improvements have been made in the grounds, which are of much beauty. A golf course has been laid out and the lake in the Park re-stocked with trout.

From the reign of Edward I. to 1455, the manor was held by the ancient Hoo family, the last of the male line being Sir Thomas Hoo, who was created Baron and K.G. for his distinguished services in the French Wars. His daughter Anne married Sir Geoffrey Boleyn, Lord Mayor of London, and gave her name to her great-grand-daughter, Anne Boleyn, the ill-fated second wife of King Henry VIII. and the mother of Queen Elizabeth.

The Napier family acquired the estate in 1601, and Sir Robert Napier, who was a favourite of James I., entertained his Sovereign at Luton Hoo in 1611. The Earl of Bute, Prime Minister of George III., bought the estate in 1762 for £111,000, and the mansion was rebuilt by Adams. Dr. Samuel Johnson visited Luton Hoo in 1781, and described it as "a very stately place indeed; the library is very splendid, and the quantity of pictures is beyond expectation—beyond hope." Shaw's fine work illustrative of "The history and antiquities of the Chapel at Luton Park," 1830, says it was of the latest and most florid period of Gothic architecture. The oak panel work and carving was

Photo by A. J. Anderson & Co., Luton.

Wardown Park.

37

Photo by A. J. Anderson & Co., Luton.

38

The Lake, Wardown Park.

Photo by A. J. Anderson & Co., Luton.

Wardown Park.

unsurpassed ; the pulpit was surmounted by a gorgeous canopy, carried up to a height of 18 feet ; the stone altar screen was also most elaborate. This ornate chapel was built by the Napiers, consecrated in 1674, and much embellished by the Bute family. The chapel and the whole interior of Luton Hoo, except the library, were destroyed in the great fire of November, 1843. The next year Lord Bute sold the property, and Mr. John Shaw Leigh purchased it in 1848. His son, Mr. J. Gerard Leigh, married the Hon. Mrs. Dudley Ward, to whom, after his death in 1875, he left the Hoo for life. Mrs. Leigh subsequently became the wife of M. de Falbe, the Danish Ambassador, and died in December, 1899.

It was Mr. Gerard Leigh who built in 1873, at a cost of £12,000 and from designs by Sir G. Street, the beautiful private chapel which is now part of the north wing of the mansion. In the apse above the altar is a splendid representation in mosaics of Christ and the Apostles in glory. The sanctuary floor is of rich marble and the panelled ceiling was painted by Italian artists, while oak canopied stalls and handsome electroliers of forty lights, recently fitted, enhance the effect of a singularly impressive interior. Sir J. Wernher has lately had erected a magnificent new organ of fifty stops by Norman and Beard, which is the finest instrument in any private chapel in the country. The Sunday services are attended by the family in residence, the household and the estate employees, a few seats being available by ticket for Luton visitors.

Miscellaneous.

WATER.

The Luton Water Company was established in 1865, and is highly prosperous. The capital outlay is represented by £134,300 consolidated ordinary stock, upon which the maximum dividend of 4 per cent. has long been paid. Besides building up a reserve fund of £8,500, the Company is this year in the position to increase its rebate to consumers to 20 per cent.—a rare and appreciated concession.

The Pumping Station is in Crescent Road, and the supply is derived from three wells bored 330 feet in the chalk, and tubed down 100 feet from the surface. There are three engines. The town has never had to complain of shortage in supply, even in times of drought. The water is pronounced by the Official Analyst to be of excellent quality. The pressure available for the hydrants is such that the Town Brigade do not require a steam fire-engine. A water-tower has been erected on each side (London Road and Hart Lane) of the hills above the town. A new ferro-concrete reservoir, containing two million gallons, has just been completed, increasing the storage capacity to $3\frac{3}{4}$ million gallons, or about four days' consumption. The mains, which measure thirty miles, have been extended to supply the villages of Leagrave and Stopsley.

The scale of charges is based on 5 per cent. of the house rental. Water is sold by meter to large consumers at 1s. to 6d. per thousand gallons, according to quantity used.

Photo by A. J. Anderson & Co., Luton.

41

Luton Hoo Mansion, West Front.

GAS.

The Luton Gas Company dates from 1834, and is equally prosperous. The capital outlay is £63,000, and dividends ranging from 10 to 4 per cent. are paid. The price is lower than in any other town in the Midlands between London and Leicester, viz., 2s. 3d. per thousand feet for private consumers and 2s. 1d. for public lighting and for gas engines of large capacity. The high quality of the gas may be gauged from the fact that its illuminating power is from 17 to 18 candles, this being in excess of the official standard.

The quantity of gas sold last year increased to nearly 300 million cubic feet and the consumers to 8,150. Gas stoves are extremely popular, the Company having 4,810 let on hire in the town.

Mr. W. R. Phillips, C.E., is the Engineer and Manager of both Companies.

ELECTRICITY.

There were some forebodings among the ratepayers when the Corporation embarked upon their electricity undertaking, but perseverance and enterprise have brought their due reward. The installation was inaugurated by Lord Kelvin, F.R.S., in July, 1901. The station is finely equipped with plant of 646 kilo-watt capacity, three Lancashire boilers and five generators. Including recent extensions, the capital outlay amounts to £43,000, and after several years of heavy deficits, the profit-earning stage has now been reached. Last year the profit was £1,206. The charges to consumers of current are cheaper than in any town of similar size, and bear favourable comparison with those of some of the largest installations in the country. The price for power and heating is from 2d. to 1d. for the largest consumers ; for light, the price is the same as for power, with the initial charge of 6d. for the first 70 hours per quarter, or consumers have the alternative of a flat rate of 4d. per unit. The average price last year, before the rate was reduced, was 2½d. ; this year it will be about 2d.

The consumers number 370, and about 22,000 lamps are connected. Nearly 21 miles of cable have been laid. Great development has taken place in the use of current for power. The engineering works of Messrs. Hayward and Tyler, the Vauxhall and West Hydraulic Company, Commercial Cars, Ltd., Brown and Green, Ltd., and Messrs. Balmforth, derive their motive power from the Corporation Works, and the extensive new works of the Davis Gas Stove Company in Dallow Road are now connected. The total supply for motive power will shortly exceed the equivalent of 1,000 h.p.

It is interesting to note that nine places of worship in Luton are lighted by electricity. Mr. W. H. Cooke, A.M.I.E.E., is the Borough Electrical Engineer.

BANKS.

There are three Banks in Luton, all situated in the main street. The first was a branch of the Hitchin and Luton Bank (Messrs. Sharples, Tuke, Lucas and Seebohm), now amalgamated with Messrs. Barclay and Co. This was first opened daily in 1839, in which year a branch of the London and County Bank was

Photo by A. J. Anderson & Co., Luton.

The Electricity Works.

Photo by A. J. Anderson, Luton.

The Grand Theatre.

established, now occupying a handsome building at the corner of Chapel Street. A branch of the Capital and Counties Bank was opened in 1898.

THEATRE.

The Grand Theatre, in Waller Street, is a handsome building of which any town of twice the size of Luton might be proud. It was opened by Mrs. Langtry in December, 1898. There is seating accommodation for a thousand people. Operatic, Shakespearean, dramatic and variety companies visit the town. Local amateurs recently gave a performance at the Theatre of Gilbert and Sullivan's " Iolanthe." The lessee is Mr. E. Graham Falcon, and the manager is Mr. L. J. Beard.

CLUBS.

The Conservative Club, Market Hill, was opened by Earl Cowper in 1893, and the Liberal Club, Manchester Street, of which Lord Battersea is President, dates from 1895. The Friendly Societies have a large Medical Institute in Waller Street with a society and family membership of 9,000.

VOLUNTEERS.

There are three Companies of the 3rd Volunteer Battalion, Bedfordshire Regiment, at Luton, under the command of Captain H. Cumberland Brown. The headquarters are at the Volunteer Club in Park Street. The Luton district also contributes members to the Imperial Yeomanry Regiments of Bedfordshire and Hertfordshire.

Photo by A. J. Anderson & Co., Luton.

The Town Hall.

MUSIC.

Luton has a flourishing Choral Society, of which Mr. F. Gostelow, F.R.C.O., A.R.A.M., A.R.C.M., is the hon. conductor. Last season, Sullivan's " Golden Legend," Cowen's " John Gilpin," and Brahms' " Song of Destiny " were performed, besides orchestral works of high standard. Sir A. C. Mackenzie and Sir J. F. Bridge have visited the town to conduct renderings of their own compositions. The Hon. Secretaries are Mr. G. H. Ordish and Mr. W. H. Eustace. The Orchestral Society, under the direction of Mr. E. E. Jeffs, has about 60 playing members. The fame of the Luton Red Cross Silver Prize Band extends far and wide. They hold the Championship Shield of the Home Counties and the South of England Cup (Hastings), while the Red Cross men have also distinguished themselves at Belle Vue, Manchester (sixth place), and the Crystal Palace (third place) in the All-England contests. The Luton Volunteer Band is of good repute, and both Corps of the Salvation Army possess bands, which take front rank in the esteem of General Booth's organization. During the past two winters, very successful series of municipal concerts have been held in the Plait Hall on Saturday evenings.

GOLF.

The royal and ancient game is popular among the business and professional men of Luton. The South Beds Golf Club has an extensive course on the Warden Hills, two miles outside the borough, where the bracing air from the wind-swept hills imparts health and vigour to the jaded townsman. The links have 18 holes, and the membership consists of about 100 gentlemen and 40 ladies. The entrance fee is : Gentlemen, £3 3s. ; ladies, 10s. 6d. ; annual subscription, £2 2s. ; visitor's green fee, 1s. per day and 5s. per month. Six trophies are offered for competition. The Captain is Mr. B. T. Crew ; Hon. Treasurer, Mr. A. F. Booth ; Hon. Secretary, Mr. F. L. Neve. The pavilion affords first-rate accommodation. The professional is J. Fletcher, who has proved an excellent club-maker and caterer. Braid and Vardon have played on the course, and expressed themselves delighted with its sporting character. The amateur record is 73 (C. H. Osborne) and the professional 67 (Vardon).

HUNTING.

The headquarters of the Hertfordshire Hunt are at Kinsbourne Green, only four miles from Luton. There are 55 couples of hounds in the pack, and meets are held four days a week, at easy access from the town. The Master is Mr. T. Fenwick Harrison, of Kingswalden Park, and W. Wells is the huntsman. The North Bucks Harriers, of which Captain S. J. Green, of Luton, is Master, is a smart pack, and the South Beds Foot Beagles, under the Mastership of Mr. R. J. K. Mott, of Ampthill Grange, are also popular. The Enfield Chase occasionally visit the district, and over the Bucks border are the Whaddon Chase and Lord Rothschild's Staghounds. The Oakley Hounds, with kennels at Milton Ernest, five miles from Bedford, mostly confine themselves to the northern half of the county.

Photo by A. J. Anderson & Co., Luton. **Warden Hills, Golf Links and Pavilion.**

SWIMMING.

The Corporation Baths are in the centre of the town, adjoining the Plait Halls. The large swimming bath is 110 feet long, and there is another bath for ladies, a number of private ones being also provided. The Town Council contemplate a scheme of enlargement. The Town Swimming Club holds the Duke of Bedford's County Cup, and arranges aquatic sports and polo matches during the season. The lake at Wardown Park is available for free bathing daily in the early morning.

CRICKET.

Some time ago it appeared as though the summer game of cricket had died a natural death until 1902, when an attempt to resuscitate the sport by the establishment of the Luton and District League was entirely successful. This organization has succeeded beyond expectations, and now each Saturday every available cricket pitch is occupied by cricket enthusiasts. The fact that over 500 players are annually registered is sufficient evidence of the revived interest in the game, and all parts of the town, on a Saturday especially, are catered for in this respect. The acquisition of Wardown Park and the consequent revival of cricket has necessitated the laying out of a first-class cricket ground, which is now second to none in the county, and is becoming a favourite spot for County matches. This ground is mostly in the hands of the Luton Town C.C., which includes all the premier players of the town, and some excellent games may be witnessed during the summer. In every stage the game is well organized in the town, and reflects credit upon all concerned.

FOOTBALL.

In the matter of football, no town of its size can boast of such a wealth of clubs and players, and this is largely due to the influence of the premier club, the Luton Town Football Club and Athletic Company, Limited. This is a strongly professional club playing football according to the Association rules, and having a most compact and well-appointed ground in Ivy Road, capable of accommodating over 10,000 spectators. During the winter months enthusiasm runs high, as the Club is engaged in the Southern and United Leagues and in the Football Association Cup competition. Besides this Club, there are about twenty-five others of a junior character, and every available space on the various recreation grounds is occupied by active participants on Saturday afternoons. The Luton Junior League attends to the needs of this class of football, and exerts a controlling force over nearly four hundred registered players. The early-closers on Wednesday afternoons have a competition in the Tradesmen's Cup, which caters for employees of the various shops and also assists charitable objects. Over all these various clubs is the ruling body, the Beds Football Association, which has its headquarters in Luton, and endeavours to wield an influence for the benefit of the game. The absence of Rugby clubs in the district tells against the ultimate success of the one Rugby club in the town, but the townspeople seem satisfied with the "soccer" game.

Fire Station.   **The Free Library.**

Photos by A. J Anderson & Co., Luton.

E

Luton in the Past.

ENOUGH has been recovered from "the deluge of Time" to show that Luton is not, as many might suppose, a modern upstart. Its history begins with the first recorded struggle in the Midlands between Saxon and Briton, and its name is the only one to be met with, besides that of Bedford, in the history of the shire for the first 350 years of Anglian rule. As the historian of Luton Church (the late Rev. H. Cobbe) says, Luton "can claim among the lords of its chief manor, besides a long succession of worthy kings, some of the foremost champions of liberty and men of the most noble character ; whilst it can show in the history and present aspect of its venerable Parish Church, with its well-authenticated succession of clergy from Saxon times to the present hour, an evidence of the continuity of the National Church, alike through changes of race and dynasty, of policies and creed, as of the still-existent beauty of one at least of her mediæval fanes."

According to the Anglo-Saxon Chronicle, " In 571, Cuthwulf fought against the Britons at Bedford and captured four towns," one of which was " Lygean-burh." As Lygea was the Roman name for the river Lea, " Lygean-burh " means " the fort on the Lea." The site of this was the circular British earthwork bordering on the source of the Lea at Leagrave, and known as " Waulud's Bank." The ditch around it was still perfect in places thirty years ago, and hundreds of Neolithic implements and arrow-heads and several British gold coins have been found there.

In 792, Offa, King of Mercia, granted by charter certain lands at Luton to St. Albans Abbey, which he had founded the year before. When King Alfred forced the invading Danes back from a large half of England and made his pact with Guthrum, he drew the frontier line across Bedfordshire—along the Lea to its source, then to Bedford and along the Ouse to Watling Street. In 895, King Alfred blockaded the Lea. As the old British " burh " or fort on the Lea fell into disuse, the increasing population created a new " tun " (enclosure) two miles away. Hence, what was formerly Lygean-burh came to be called " Lygetun " as early as Offa's Charter. In 914, an army of the Danes were put to flight by the men of Luton. The expedition came down Watling Street to Dunstable, and then along the ancient British track, known as the Icknield Way, which crosses the Lea in the middle of Limbury.

There is evidence that Luton was a Royal Manor before the tenth century. King Athelstan, one of our best Saxon Kings, and grandson of Alfred the Great, held at Luton an important Witanegemot, or National Parliament, in 931. The place is called " Leowton " in the charter, and Bishop Stubbs assigns this to Luton. Two Welsh princes and a hundred notables, making one of the largest attendances on record, were present. There was a considerable Saxon population at Luton, according to Domesday Book, 1086. It states that in Edward the Confessor's reign, Morcar had been priest at Luton, but William the Chamberlain then held the church from the Conqueror. The Domesday entry shows six mills in " Loitone " yielding 100 shillings

Photo by A. J. Anderson & Co., Luton.

Bute Hospital.

51

and " wood for 2,000 swine " (the largest in the county). Luton was among the earliest episcopally constituted Vicarages, and John de St. Albans, 1220, was the first of a long list, some fifty in number, of Vicars of Luton.

Local Notabilities.

KINGS, nobles and eminent men have "left footprints on the sands of time " in the Royal Manor of Luton, which go far to make an epitome of English history. Alone of the Kings who owned the Manor, Athelstan resided for a time at Luton, and the holding of the Witanegemot here nearly a thousand years ago was probably the occasion of the consecration of the Saxon church. Henry I. bestowed lands in Luton on Robert Earl of Gloucester, who championed the cause of his half-sister, Matilda, against King Stephen. Earl Robert built the Early Norman church at Luton. Simon de Montfort, " The Founder of the English House of Commons," held the Manor of Luton for twenty-seven years as part of the dowry of his wife, the Lady Eleanor, sister of Henry III. The notorious rebel Baron, Fawkes de Breauté, Sheriff of seven counties, was lord of the manor of Luton for seven years. In 1224, Fawkes was brought to book by the King's Justices at Dunstable for various offences, one of which was the seizure of lands belonging to 32 Freemen of Luton, where he had built a castle at the south-east corner of Luton churchyard. The great siege of Bedford Castle, where Fawkes de Breauté had imprisoned one of the Judges,

ended the career of this lawless chief of John's foreign mercenaries.

An echo of Magna Charta days comes from Biscot, a hamlet of Luton. The manor of Biscot was owned by Robert Fitzwalter, the leader of the Barons' confederacy against King John. By the way, the Barons met near Luton, under the pretext of a tournament, to concert a plan of operations. For nearly two centuries the Manor of Luton was in the hands of the family and descendants of William Marshall, Earl of Pembroke, who was Regent after the death of King John. In 1416, it reverted to the Crown, and was granted by Henry V. to his brother, John Duke of Bedford, during whose government as Regent of the English territories in France the heroic Maid of Orleans inspired to victory the armies of the Dauphin, Charles VII.

Another lord of the manor played a prominent part in the Wars of the Roses. Lord Wenlock, though many honours had been given him by Edward IV., went over to the Lancastrians, and was chosen by Queen Margaret to command the centre at the great battle of Tewkesbury, 1471, where he was slain. Lord Wenlock had held the responsible post of Captain-Governor of Calais. The Wenlock family contributed three representatives of the shire in Parliament.

Late in the fifteenth century, Adrian Castello, an Italian, who became a Cardinal and an aspirant to the Papacy, was thrust into the living of Luton. Queen Elizabeth owned the Rectorial tithes of Luton for forty years. Sir Robert Napier, a Scotch favourite of King James I., who knighted him at Luton Hoo in

Photo by A. J. Anderson & Co., Luton.

The Children's Home.

1611, was given the advowson of the living and the Manor of Luton.

The author of " Pilgrim's Progress " was probably an occasional preacher at Luton. George Fox, the apostle of the Quakers, paid four visits to Luton, and John Wesley preached here six times. John Pomfret, the poet, was born in Luton Vicarage.

The Crawley family, who are still the chief landowners, provided two Barons of the Exchequer in the seventeenth century.

The Earl of Bute, Prime Minister of George III., resided at Luton Hoo, and a description of Dr. Johnson's visit there in 1783 is given in Boswell's " Life of Samuel Johnson." Lord Bute's youngest son, the Hon. Wm. Stuart, D.D., was Vicar of Luton for seventeen years. He married the last surviving grand-daughter of William Penn, the founder of Pennsylvania, and became afterwards Archbishop of Armagh and Primate of Ireland. Both are buried in Luton Church. Boswell refers to Dr. Stuart as "an exemplary parish priest." While occupying the chair of St. Patrick, he was a munificent reliever of the poor during one of the many famines in Ireland and built schools and parsonages in his diocese.

Of special interest also to American visitors is the fact that in 1660 Lawrence Washington, grand-uncle of the famous George Washington, married Mary Jones, of Luton, in Luton Church, and their child was baptised there.

The present Bishop of Ely (Dr. Chase) is descended from an old Luton family, one of whom was a local surgeon and the other a solicitor.

The office of High Sheriff of Bedfordshire is filled for the first time this year by a native and resident of Luton in the person of Mr. J. W. Green, of The Larches.

The Flora of Luton District.

BY JAMES SAUNDERS, A.L.S.

THE district in which Luton is situated lies upon the upper beds of the cretaceous series. The town itself is chiefly upon the middle chalk, the hills on each side being capped by chalk-rock and the base of the upper chalk, over which lies an extensive deposit of clay, with flints, bearing evidence of a marine origin.

The most noteworthy section in the vicinity of Luton is an exposure of two seams of chalk-rock, which is visible in a cutting on the Midland Railway about a mile and a half south-east of the town. It has been frequently examined by experts, who have found it to contain numerous relics of marine organisms, most of which have figured in various geological publications. The lowest parts of the Luton Valley are about 350 feet above sea level, the hills on each side rising a few yards above the 500 feet contour.

It will readily be understood that, as the whole district has a sub-stratum of chalk, those native plants that affect a limestone soil will be well represented. This is particularly the case upon those hills, on which the ancient greensward has never been disturbed by

Photo by A. J. Anderson & Co., Luton.

Park Road Bridge.

the plough, such as Warden Hills, Barton Hills, and Blows Downs. Noteworthy representatives of this ancient flora are certain orchids, which in some seasons are so abundant as to affect the general tone of the hillsides. It will suffice to mention Bee Orchis, Fly Orchis, Dwarf Orchis, Fragrant Orchis, Pyramidal Orchis, the Spotted Orchis, and Autumn Ladies' Tresses. In the adjoining coppices, white Helleborine and broad leaved Helleborine can be found, in addition to which are the commoner forms of the early spring orchids. Other rare plants on these hills are the Anemone Pulsatilla, Mountain Cudweed, and the Dane's Milk-Vetch (Astragalus danicus).

At Limbury and in Luton Hoo Park, the Danewort or Dwarf Elder grows, with which is associated the legend that it is only to be found where Danish blood has been spilt. An irruption of the Danes took place in 914 A.D. in this district. In Stow's History it is stated, "The Danes invaded Herts near to Ligeton (Luton), slew many and took much spoil." They were defeated in this neighbourhood in 915 by King Edward, so that historical records give some colour to the legend.

The nearest place to Luton where the insect-eating plants called Sundews are to be found is Flitwick Marsh, which is nine miles distant by the Midland Railway.

Of the agrarian weeds, a remarkable one is the Large Earth-nut, which is quite distinct from the Small Earth-nut. In its distribution it is limited to the Eastern counties. A century ago, it was not known in Bedfordshire, but it has invaded this district from the East, is gradually spreading across the county, and has passed the borders of Bucks. It is particularly abundant in chalky fields in the Limbury and Leagrave district. Pigs are fond of its tubers, which are said to have an intoxicating effect upon the animals when first turned into the fields where these plants are abundant.

Of the less known forms of organic life that interest biologists, the Mycetozoa may be specified. This group of organisms is one of the many that lie on the borderland between plants and animals. The district around Luton has been proved to be peculiarly rich in them, both in numbers and in species. The researches of a few enthusiasts who live in this neighbourhood have resulted in the discovery of nearly one hundred well defined species within a reasonable distance of Luton. As the British Museum authorities recognise only two hundred and seven species for the whole world, it is evident either that this locality is especially rich in these forms or that it has been searched with exceptional care.

The neighbourhood of Luton would amply repay the investigations of those who are interested in Nature studies, whether they are geological, botanical, or biological, and the antiquarian would also find many subjects which would well reward original research.

Places to Visit.

DUNSTABLE (5 miles).—At the ancient Priory Church in 1533 Catharine of Aragon's sentence of divorce was pronounced by Archbishop Cranmer. The broad High Street is part of the Roman Watling Street. The breezy Downs (a spur of the Chilterns) and the Knolls at Totternhoe, near which is a British encampment called Maiden-Bower, attract many holiday-makers.

HARPENDEN (6 miles).—An extensive Common, the scene of an annual race-meeting. Here is the famous Rothamsted agricultural experiment station, the oldest in the world. A mile distant is Mackrye End, associated with Charles Lamb.

BARTON (6 miles).—Picturesque spring and hills above the Church. Beautiful views also from Markham Hills, Sharpenhoe, and Lilley Hoo within a short distance.

ASHRIDGE (12 miles).—The estate of Earl Brownlow. In the park is a lofty monument to the Duke of Bridgwater, "The Father of Inland Navigation." Adjoining is Aldbury, the residence of Mrs. Humphrey Ward.

AYOT (9 miles).—Amongst some of the prettiest Hertfordshire scenery and near to Brocket Hall, where Lord Melbourne resided and Lord Palmerston died.

AMPTHILL (12 miles).—The Park, which is the property of the Duke of Bedford and the residence of Emily Lady Ampthill, contains some of the most venerable oak trees in England, two being 36 feet in circumference. A stone cross marks the site of Ampthill Castle, the retreat of Queen Catharine during her trial.

SILSOE (10 miles).—Wrest Park, the property of Lord Lucas, and now occupied by the Hon. Whitelaw Reid, the American Ambassador. Gardens open on Thursdays ; the park is always open to pedestrians.

FLITTON (11 miles).—Adjoining the Parish Church is the Mausoleum of the De Grey family, consisting of four chambers ; magnificent marble effigies, mural tablets and monuments of the Dukes of Kent.

OLD WARDEN (18 miles).—A beautiful model village and favourite spot for picnics ; remarkable carved oak pews in the church.

HITCHIN (10 miles).—An old market town, on the outskirts of which is the new Garden City at Letchworth.

WOBURN SANDS (15 miles).—A health resort, surrounded by lovely pine and fir woods, through which are public paths.

Someries Castle, near Luton.

WOBURN (13 miles).—The seat of the Duke of Bedford, K.G. The main road passes through the Park, in which can be seen a remarkable collection of wild animals—such as Chinese and Japanese deer, antelopes, elk, blackbuck, llamas, emus and rheas, besides all kinds of swans and water-birds. An imposing Sculpture Gallery is attached to the Abbey. The new parish church of St. Mary, built by the eighth Duke of Bedford, at a cost of £35,000, has in its tower the heaviest bell in Bedfordshire, 55 cwts. The present Duke has presented a beautiful reredos and new organ.

HATFIELD (12 miles).—The historic estate and mansion of the Marquis of Salisbury.

LEIGHTON BUZZARD (12 miles).—Fine collegiate church; ancient Market Cross in the High Street. Within two miles are Ascott, the estate of Mr. Leopold de Rothschild, and Mentmore, the residence of the Earl of Rosebery, K.G. Both are occasionally open to visitors.

————

(It is only necessary to mention that St. Albans, with its Cathedral, and Bedford, with its Schools, river, and Bunyan and Howard associations, require about half-an-hour's train journey).

HERBERT STALKER,

Printer, Stationer,   Telephone No. 49y.
Bookseller and Newsagent.

Every description of PRINTING at moderate charges.

A large Stock of Account Books, Commercial and Fancy Stationery, Bibles, Prayers, Hymn Books, Purses, Card Cases, Wallets, &c.

19, Wellington St., Luton.

" THE FRANKLIN "

Temperance Commercial Hotel and Restaurant.

Telegrams—"The Franklin, Luton."

THIS HOTEL AND RESTAURANT supplies the great need of the town of Luton, conducted as it is on strictly Temperance Principles; supplying the very best of Provisions, the quality of which, combined with strict cleanliness and Moderate Charges, cannot be surpassed.

PRIVATE DINING ROOMS.

LARGE OR SMALL PARTIES.
CYCLIST'S, CRICKET, FOOTBALL, HOCKEY, TENNIS OR GOLF PARTIES.

Good Commercial House.

Close to the Town Hall,

George St., LUTON

Five Minutes from the Stations.

J. C. LEWIS, Proprietor.

Wootton & Webb,

Members of the Pharmaceutical Society of Great Britain.

Chemists, ❧

Established 1837.
TELEPHONE No. **0644.**

Market Place, Luton.

Raw Drugs vary considerably in potency, as is well known. Wherever possible we use preparations standardized to contain known percentages of active principles, thus ensuring uniformity of results.

TRUSSES, ENEMA AND OTHER SYRINGES, ELASTIC STOCKINGS, HOT WATER BOTTLES AND ALL SURGICAL AND INVALIDS' REQUISITES KEPT IN STOCK.

PATENT MEDICINES AT STORE PRICES.

ALL PRESCRIPTIONS ENTRUSTED TO OUR CARE ARE COMPOUNDED BY DULY QUALIFIED CHEMISTS ONLY.

Strange & Co.'s

TAILORING IS THE BEST.

Unequalled for Gent.s' and Juvenile Suits and Overcoats, READY-MADE OR TO MEASURE.

The LARGEST VARIETY and the BEST VALUE in the town and district.

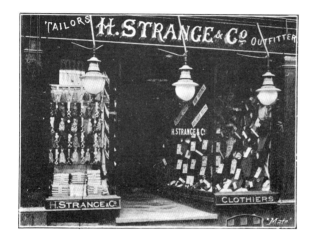

The Popular Tailors & Outfitters.

ESTABLISHED 1842.

LOWEST CASH PRICES.

AN IMMENSE STOCK OF CHOICE GOODS IN HOSIERY, SHIRTS, TIES, HATS, GLOVES, WATERPROOFS, UMBRELLAS, RUGS, &c.

38, Wellington St., Luton,

And at ST. ALBANS,

ST. GREGORY'S SCHOOL,
THE DOWNS, LUTON.

Principal: **WM. HOUSE,**

BALLIOL COLLEGE, OXFORD.

Healthily situated at the end of the Chiltern Hills, 600 feet above sea level.

The School House is fitted throughout with electrict light, well ventilated, and the sanitary arrangements are perfect.

Boys are received between the ages of 7 and 14, and thoroughly prepared for the Public Schools.

FEES MODERATE AND INCLUSIVE.

Large Playing Fields
for Cricket, Football and Hockey.

Boys attend the Town Swimming Baths twice a week during the Summer Term.

Prospectus on application to the Principal.

Luton High School for Girls and :: :: Kindergarten.

Recognised by Board of Education under Regs. 3 & 4 of Schedule.

PRINCIPAL:—

MISS GILFILLAN

(REG. COL. B.),

Assisted by **MISS HUTTON**

(daughter of Rev. W. J. Hutton).

THIS SCHOOL provides a sound Education on **High School Lines,** including Latin and Modern Languages, Mathematics and Nature Study, as well as **Physical Exercise** in the form of Drill and Out-door Games.

Pupils are prepared for **Cambridge Local** and other public exams., and if they wish to follow the profession of **Secondary School Teachers,** they can continue their studies and prepare for **Cambridge Higher Local,** or **London Matric.,** etc., in the School.

The Head Mistress of the High School is a University Graduate, while

The Kindergarten is under a fully trained certificated Mistress, who can also undertake the training of Students for the Nat. Frœbel Union Exams.

Boys' Preparatory Class.

A limited number of **Full and Weekly Boarders** are received at

LYNDHURST, CARDIFF ROAD.

Terms from 10 to 18 guineas per term. Prospectus, etc., on application.

F

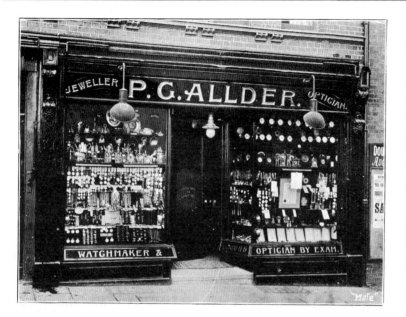

WHEN buying Jewellery, beauty of design, fine workmanship, high quality and low prices are the points which are looked for.

These are the chief characteristics of my stock, and you only need to pay me a visit in order to quickly realise this.

Call & see the exquisite examples of the Jeweller's Art I am now exhibiting.

Worth Noting.

When your Watch requires cleaning, or your glasses are broken, bring them to me. I will attend to them promptly, give you careful, conscientious service, and charge you only a moderate price.

I am a fully qualified Ophthalmic Optician, holding the Diplomas of the Spectacle Makers' Company, and the British Optical Association.

I have a Sight Testing Room, equipped with every appliance demanded by modern Optical Science, and can guarantee accuracy and satisfaction.

P. G. ALLDER

D.B.O.A., F.S.M.C.

Optician & Jeweller,

21, Park Square,

LUTON.

W. L. GATES,

Telephone
62.

Telephone
62.

HIGH CLASS FAMILY **GROCER.**

FURNISHING & BUILDERS' **IRONMONGER.**

W. & A. GILBEY'S WINES and SPIRITS.

GRATES, STOVES, RANGES.
TOOLS FOR ALL TRADES.

❧ 49, 51, George Street, LUTON. ❧

W. A. SALE & Co., *Cycle & Motor Engineers.*

Accessories

Motor Petrol.
Carbide.
Oils. Grease.

* : * *

Accumulators
Charged.

* * *

Cycle Lamps,
Bells, Pumps,
Tyres, etc.

Repairs

and

Alterations

by Expert
Mechanics.

* * *

AGENTS FOR

"**Singer,**"
"**Quadrant,**"

and all best makes
of Cycles.

70, GEORGE STREET, LUTON.

H. J. WELLS,

6 and 8, New Bedford Road, LUTON.

Wholesale and Retail

Bedding Manufacturer, Upholsterer and Cabinet Maker.

PICTURE FRAMING and MOUNT CUTTING in all its branches.

Trade supplied with Mouldings, etc.

—— Cheapest House for ——
Feathers, Millpuffs and Flocks.

Bedding Purified by Machinery.
Overmantels a Speciality.

**Repairs in all its Branches. All Work
done on the premises.**

F. COOK,

TAILOR and OUTFITTER,

1, High Town Rd., LUTON.

Drop us a Postcard,

From any distance, we will immediately attend to your requirements.

GALE & SON,

Complete :: :: House Furnishers,

15, High Town Road, and 12, Chapel Street, Luton.

ESTIMATES REMOVALS FREE

Cabinet Makers, Upholsterers and Bedding Manufacturers.

BLINDS OF EVERY DESCRIPTION MADE AND FITTED,

CARPETS AND LINOS LAID FREE OF CHARGE.

T. WOOD & SONS,

—— Decorators & Plumbers, ——
Hot Water & Electrical Engineers.

LEAD BURNERS.   ALL KINDS OF REPAIRS UNDERTAKEN.

ARTISTIC DECORATING IN ALL
ITS BRANCHES.

ESTABLISHED OVER **40** YEARS.   TELEPHONE NO. **19.**

SOLE AGENTS FOR THE DISTRICT FOR:—

—— THE CARMIEN PORTABLE GAS ——

AND

THE FORBES & BRITISH PURE ACETYLENE
GAS Co., Ltd.

PARTICULARS ON APPLICATION.

21, Chapel Street, LUTON.

——HALL & SON,——

Chemists and Druggists.

**Proprietors of Metaphosphine, the sure Cough Cure.   Aerated
Water Manufacturers.   Toilet Requisites, etc.**

ESTABLISHED **1821.**   TELEPHONE NO. **248X1.**

Patent Medicines at Store Prices for Cash.

Medicines prepared with purest Drugs and Dispensed by Qualified Assistants.

George Street, & High Town Road, LUTON.

G

St. Dominic's Convent,

ROTHESAY ROAD, LUTON,
BEDFORDSHIRE.

Boarding School for the Daughters of Gentlemen.

WITHIN 35 minutes of London; and situated nearly 500 feet above sea
level. Healthy situation. Bracing air. Extensive grounds and Tennis.
Superior Education. All modern accomplishments. Pupils prepared for Public
Examinations by Certificated English and Foreign Teachers. Special facilities
for Modern Languages.

Private Lessons in French, Piano, Harmonium, Singing, Drawing,
Painting, Embossed Leather, Scientific Dressmaking and Embroidery.

High School and Kindergarten (adjoining the Convent).

A few Lady Boarders received. Daily Mass. Benediction twice a week
in the Convent's Chapel.

Little Boy's received as Boarders in a separate Department.

Apply to the **REV. MOTHER PRIORESS.**

A. P. PEPPER,

Cycle Agent

38, CHAPEL STREET,
LUTON.

H. H. MOWER

Tool Merchant, Cutler and Ironmonger.

PARK SQUARE, LUTON.

Speciality :
Best Warranted Tools of every description at Exceptionally Low Prices.

Telephone 0611.

HILL & WOOD,

Electrical and General ENGINEERS,

Chapel Street, LUTON.   MOTOR CAR AGENTS.

ELECTRIC LIGHT AND POWER ENGINEERS.

If your Car breaks down

Give us a call and we will put you straight. We can supply the smallest bolt to an Engine or Gear Box.

The Oldest and Best Paper in Luton.
Estab. 1855.

Circulates in over 50 Towns and Villages in Beds, Bucks and Herts.

Published every Friday Morning—ONE PENNY.
Advertisements received up to Thursday afternoon.

Publishers : E. J. ATKINS & SON,

54, George Street, LUTON.

Nat. Tel. 0651.

Telegrams—"Worsley, Engineer, Luton." Established 1886.

C. J. WORSLEY,

— ENGINEER. —

HEAT, LIGHT AND ELECTRIC, STEAM,
—— POWER. —— GAS & WATER.

MELSON ST., LUTON.

Speciality: STRAW & FELT HAT MACHINERY.

MATE'S ILLUSTRATED GUIDES.

Printed and Published by W. MATE & SONS LTD.,
BOURNEMOUTH.

BOURNEMOUTH,	NEW FOREST,
CANARY ISLAND,	NORTH OF IRELAND,
CHRISTCHURCH,	PLYMOUTH,
FOLKESTONE,	SALISBURY,
GLASGOW AND	SCARBOROUGH,
WEST OF SCOTLAND,	SOUTHAMPTON,
ISLE OF MAN,	SOUTHSEA,
ISLE OF WIGHT,	VENTNOR.

All 1s each, Post Free 1s. 4d.

Aberdeen,	Exeter,	Rugby,
Axe Valley,	Exmouth,	Saltburn & Redcar
Bangor,	Herne Bay,	Sandown,
Barnstaple,	Honiton,	Seaton,
Barry & Barry	Ilfracombe,	Shanklin,
Dock,	Keswick,	Sherborne,
Bedford,	Lake District,	Sidmouth,
Bideford,	Launceston,	Skegness,
Blackpool,	Malvern,	Southampton,
Bodmin,	Margate,	Southend,
Bridlington,	Marlborough,	St. Albans,
Bridport,	Matlock,	St. Austell,
Budleigh	Minehead,	Swanage,
Salterton,	Morpeth,	Teignmouth,
Burnham,	Newbury,	Tenby,
Buxton,	Newquay,	Thames Valley,
Camborne,	Newton Abbot,	Tiverton,
Cambridge,	Okehampton,	Tonbridge,
Cardigan Bay,	Oxford	Trowbridge,
Chard,	Peak District,	Tunbridge Wells,
Cleethorpes,	Penarth,	Tynemouth,
Clevedon,	Penzance,	Ventnor,
Colwyn Bay,	Ramsgate,	Weymouth,
Cork & South of	Reading,	Whitby,
Ireland,	Redruth,	Winchester,
Dawlish,	Reigate & Redhill,	York.
Devizes,	Rhyl,	

*Each containing about 100 pages   Royal 8vo. oblong, with about
50 High-Class Photographic Process Views.   Price 6d. each, Post Free. 9d.*

W. ROWNTREE & SONS,

Established in the Reign of King George III.

Scarborough,

And at YORK.

House and Estate Agents,

Send for Particulars of the best FURNISHED and UNFURNISHED HOUSES.

✿ ✿ ✿

House Furnishers, China and Glass Merchants.

REMOVAL & STORAGE CONTRACTORS.

A Series of FURNISHED ROOMS with original designs in Furniture and Decoration, on the first floor.

The Post Order Department

is under the personal supervision of members of the firm.
Orders are despatched by the next Mail or Train following the receipt of the order.

A full range of Patterns and Sketches free on application. Carriage paid on all Orders of £1 and upwards throughout the United Kingdom.

DRESSMAKERS,
Milliners,
Ladies' Tailors,
Gentlemen's Outfitters.

Mourning Orders
Promptly attended to.

TEA AND WRITING ROOM

ON THE GROUND FLOOR.

Scarborough, the most charming Health Resort.

COOL IN SUMMER.   MILD IN WINTER.

COCKERMOUTH, KESWICK and PENRITH RAILWAY.

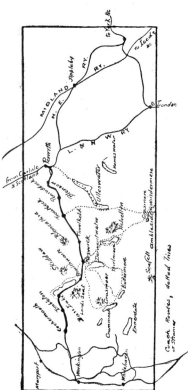

EXTENSIVE THROUGH TRAIN SERVICE and **THROUGH BOOKING ARRANGEMENTS** with all principal places.

TOURIST TICKETS from all parts to **KESWICK** and **TROUTBECK** (for **ULLSWATER**).

CIRCULAR TOUR TICKETS from Euston and other Stations to **LAKE DISTRICT**, including **KESWICK & WINDERMERE**.

WEEK-END and **TEN DAY TICKETS** from L. & N.W., L. & Y., N. E., and Midland Stations.

During Summer Months the following Excursion arrangements :

WEEKLY EXCURSIONS to and from **LONDON**.

CIRCULAR TOURS over all parts of **LAKE DISTRICT**.

PLEASURE PARTY TICKETS, etc., etc.

P. THOMPSON,
Secretary & General Manager.

BUXTON, DERBYSHIRE.

Buxton Hydropathic

Telegraphic Address :
"COMFORTABLE, BUXTON."

National Telephone
No. **5.**

SITUATED over one thousand feet above the Sea Level. Sheltered from the North and East. Overlooking the Public — Gardens, and close to the — celebrated Mineral Wells and Baths.

HYDROPATHIC BATHS of every description, Electric Baths, Massage, Electro-Massage, and the Nauheim Treatment.

Cinderella Dance every Saturday.
Concert every Sunday.

Magnificent Public Rooms.
American Elevator.
Electric Light.

H. LOMAS, Managing Director.

Chatsworth, Residential Hotel and Boarding Establishment,

OPEN ALL THE YEAR.

SANDOWN BAY, ISLE OF WIGHT.

Chatsworth is a well appointed and newly decorated Establishment. Handsome Public Rooms, Comfortable Smoke Room and Cosy Lounge, Spacious Corridors, Splendid Recreation Room, Parquet Flooring. Electric Light throughout. Baths—Hot and Cold. Good Cycle Accommodation (Lock up). Every Home Comfort.

BOATING AND BATHING EXCELLENT.

Private Grounds for Lawn Tennis and Croquet. Sanitary arrangements are of the most modern and perfect description. Certificate.

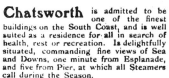

Chatsworth is admitted to be one of the finest buildings on the South Coast, and is well suited as a residence for all in search of health, rest or recreation. Is delightfully situated, commanding fine views of Sea and Downs, one minute from Esplanade, and five from Pier, at which all Steamers call during the Season.

THE CHATSWORTH OMNIBUS meets all trains. Fine Golf Links within easy distance. Coaches leave Chatsworth daily during the Season for excursions to all parts of Interest.

Special Winter Terms from 51/6 inclusive.

Moderate and Illustrated Tariff on application. Nat. Telephone No. 0191.

Misses Jannings & Catt, Proprietresses.

BELFAST.

Grand Central Hotel.

The Finest Hotel in Ireland.

200 :: Rooms.

Electric Light throughout.

Passenger Lifts to all Floors

Most Central Position.

Excellent Cuisine.

Moderate Tariff.

Omnibuses from the Hotel attend the arrival and departure of all Steamers and Trains.

TELEGRAMS: "GRAND CENTRAL," BELFAST.

Cook's Coupons accepted.

London and North Western Railway.

FROM AND TO BOURNEMOUTH VIA WATERLOO AND EUSTON.

QUICKEST AND MOST COMFORTABLE ROUTE

Between **LONDON** (EUSTON) and BIRMINGHAM, MANCHESTER, LIVERPOOL, NORTH WALES and the ENGLISH LAKE DISTRICT.

West Coast Royal Mail Route
BETWEEN
ENGLAND and SCOTLAND

LONDON (EUSTON) AND	EDINBURGH	IN 8 HOURS.
	GLASGOW	„ 8 „
	ABERDEEN	„ 11¼ „
	INVERNESS	„ 13.10

Breakfast, Luncheon, Dining and Sleeping Cars.

FREQUENT OMNIBUS SERVICE BETWEEN WATERLOO & EUSTON.

EUSTON, 1905.

Most Convenient and Expeditious Train and Steamboat Services
BETWEEN
ENGLAND and IRELAND

Via Holyhead and Greenore, Dublin (North Wall) or Kingstown.

Via Fleetwood, Liverpool, Belfast and Londonderry.

Via Carlisle, Stranraer, and Larne.

FREDERICK HARRISON,
GENERAL MANAGER.

From Dr. A. B. GRIFFITHS, F.R.S., (Edin.), F.C.S.

Member of the Chemical Societies of Paris and St. Petersburg; Lecturer on Chemistry Central School of Chemistry and Pharmacy; Analytical Chemist and Assayer; Consulting Chemist to National Amateur Gardeners' Association; Diplome de l'Institut de France (l'Academie des Sciences); Bacteriological and Agricultural Expert; Agricultural Analyst for the County Soke of Peterborough.

12, Knowle Road, BRIXTON,
London, *March 17th, 1896.*

I hereby certify that I have examined **Ross's "Royal Belfast Ginger Ale,"** and find that it is a genuine preparation and contains nothing that is injurious. It is, in fact, a salutary, palatable and invigorating beverage—being made of materials of absolute purity. It possesses a flavour and bouquet which render it quite unique. I can conscientiously state that **Ross's "Royal Belfast Ginger Ale"** is a wholesome delicious drink, possessing sustaining and invigorating qualities. It is the **finest Ginger Ale** I have ever examined.

A. B. GRIFFITHS, Ph. D.

OF
STORES, CHEMISTS,
AND
ROWLAND'S,
67, Hatton Garden,
LONDON.

SOFT FAIR SKIN

A beautiful Complexion, and Face, Hands and Arms of matchless whiteness

ARE ENSURED TO THOSE WHO USE

Rowland's Kalydor

which preserves it from all the trying changes of weather,

REMOVES REDNESS

and roughness, soothes and heals all Cutaneous Eruptions, renders the Skin beautifully

SOFT AND SMOOTH

and imparts a matchless beauty to the complexion unattainable by any other means. Warranted harmless. Bottles, 2/3 and 4/6.

MIDLAND RAILWAY.

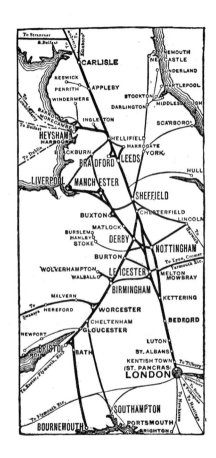

The Best Route

FOR COMFORTABLE TRAVEL AND PICTURESQUE SCENERY

TO AND FROM THE

HOLIDAY RESORTS

OF

DERBYSHIRE, THE NORFOLK COAST, THE LANCASHIRE COAST,
YORKSHIRE SPAS AND WATERING PLACES,
THE SOUTH AND WEST OF ENGLAND,
ALL PARTS OF SCOTLAND,
THE ISLE OF MAN AND THE NORTH OF IRELAND.

THE NEW EXPRESS ROUTE, VIA HEYSHAM,

TO AND FROM THE

ISLE OF MAN AND NORTH OF IRELAND.

Magnificent new steamers Sail Daily (Sundays excepted) between HEYSHAM and BELFAST, and during the season between HEYSHAM and DOUGLAS in connection with Express Trains from and to all parts of the Midland System

Trains arrive and depart alongside Steamers at Heysham. Luggage transferred free of charge.

For Programmes of Cheap Tickets, apply to any Midland Station Master or District Superintendent, or to MR. J. ELLIOTT, Superintendent of the Line, Derby.

DERBY.

JOHN MATHIESON, General Manager.